Silver
Jewelry Treasures

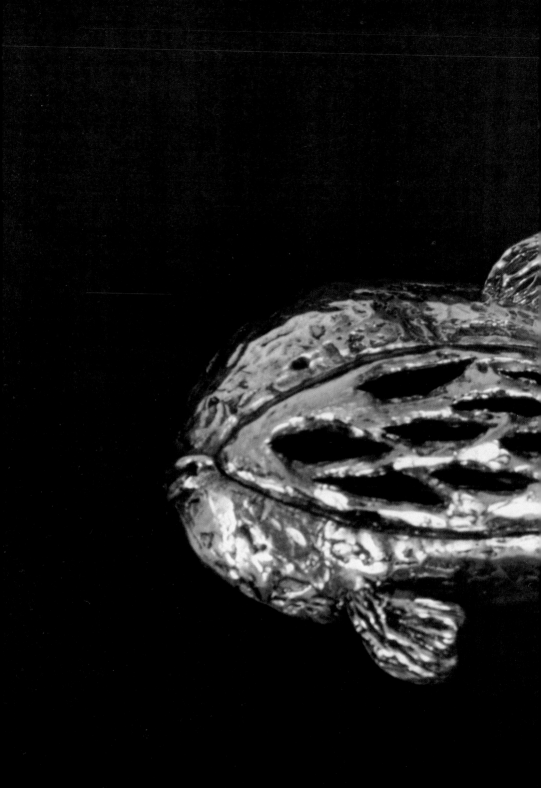

SILVER
Jewelry Treasures

Nancy N. Schiffer

Schiffer Publishing Ltd

77 Lower Valley Road, Atglen, PA 19310

ACKNOWLEDGMENTS

Sincere appreciation is extended to the following people who contributed in many ways to the completion of this book. Collectors Adeline Trievel, Peggy Ann Osborne, Beebe Hopper, Angela Kramer, Jean Nawodylo, Ted Garoutte and a wonderful couple who prefer to remain anonymous all shared their silver treasures for photography.

Jewelry designers Terry Schreiner Albert of Shriner Jewelry and William de Lillo and Robert F. Clark of Wm. de Lillo USA opened their archives and explained the processes and materials they used in detail.

Jewelry dealers Carole A. Berk of Bethesda, Maryland; Sandy De Maio of Bryn Mawr, Pennsylvania; Mim Klein of Philadelphia; Lynn Trusdell of Crown & Eagle Antiques in New Hope, Pennsylvania; Elsa Zukin and Joan Toborowski of E. & J. Rothstein Antiques in West Chester, Pennsylvania; Jackie Fleischmann, Dennis Cogdell, and Francis Cronin of the Black Angus Antiques Mall in Adamstown, Pennsylvania; Muriel Karasik, Malvina Solomon, Michael Greenberg, Nora Lee at Bizarre Bazaar, and Norman Crider in New York; Linda Morgan in New York and London; Tanya Hunter and Veronica Manussis of Cobra & Bellamy, Sonja and David Newell-Smith of Tadema Gallery, Lawrence Feldman of Fior, and Christie's in London; Mary Kathryn Harris at Turquoise Lady and Guy Berger at the Palms Trading Company in Albuquerque, New Mexico; Tom Wheeler at Hogback Trading Company in Waterflow, New Mexico; and Bruce MaGee at the Beyond Tradition gallery in Holbrook, Arizona. Thank you all for your sustaining interest and contributions.

Printed in the United States of America
ISBN: 0-88740-458-8

Published by Schiffer Publishing, Ltd.
77 Lower Valley Road
Atglen, PA 19310
Please write for a free catalog.
This book may be purchased from the publisher.
Please include $2.95 postage.
Try your bookstore first.

We are interested in hearing from authors
with book ideas on related subjects.

Title page:
Double Fish brooch in sterling silver and vermeil, designed by Robert F. Clark for Wm. de Lillo Ltd., c. 1973. Wm. de Lillo Archive.

Contents

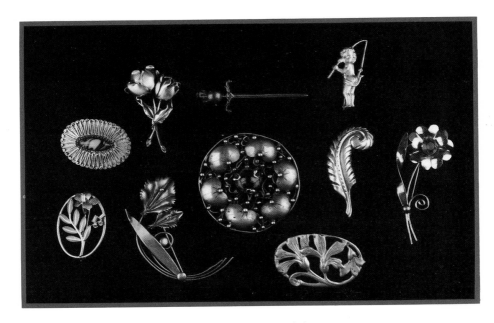

Brooches of sterling and plated silver from the mid-twentieth
century.

Silver Jewelry Treasures

Treasures of silver jewelry have delighted mankind for thousands of years. The lustrous white color and malleability of the precious metal, and its widespread distribution have made silver a practical choice for jewelry adornment in diverse cultures.

A fairly abundant element, silver is found in pockets dispursed throughout the world. Pure silver is mined primarily in Mexico, The United States (in order of volume by states: in Idaho, Utah, Montana, Arizona, Colorado, Nevada, California, Texas and New Mexico), in Canada (Ontario and British Columbia), Peru, India, Japan, and Australia. It is found with deposits of copper in Germany and alloyed with other metals such as gold, mercury, and copper in other regions. Because it is easily available today, silver is affordable in the developed societies of the world.

Whether through discovery or trade, silver has been available to artisans from the earliest days of civilization. Ornamental articles of silver turn up in ancient sites, and references appear in the world's earliest literature. The ancient Hebrews knew silver by a name meaning *pale*. The name the ancient Greeks gave silver meant *shining*. And the chemical symbol for silver, Ag, comes from its Latin name, *argent*.

Silver is harder than gold, but softer than copper. It can be hammered into remarkably thin sheets and drawn into wire finer than human hair.

Silver is not changed by moisture, dryness, alkalies, or vegetable acids. However, sulfur, or air that contains sulfur, will cause silver to turn black. Therefore, silver tarnishes very quickly in places where coal gas, which contains sulfur, is present.

Pure silver is too soft to withstand constant wear, so it usually is mixed with copper to form an alloy before it is made into useful objects. The copper-silver alloy is used by silversmiths to make coins, jewelry, and tableware. *Sterling* silver contains at least 925 parts pure silver out of a thousand, and often more. The word *sterling* has been used to mean high quaility silver since the 1200s. At that time, the coins of England had decreased in value and contained little silver. The only coins that contained large proportions of silver were those coined by the merchants of the Hanseatic league in northern Germany. These coins were called *Easterlings* to distinguish them from the low-silver alloy coins of England. English speech quickly turned *Easterlings* into *sterling*. Because its color is likened to moonbeams, silver is astrologically the metal of the moon.

Besides silver jewelry ornaments, in modern time tableware of great quantity is made with silver. Silver has been widely used in surgery and dentistry because it does not tarnish easily. In photography, compounds of silver are used for purposes ranging from coating the film to developing it. The photographic industry is the world's largest user of silver.

The early silver jewelry trade in America grew gradually with colonization in the eighteenth century. In coastal towns, blacksmiths did a bit of work in silver, but only the larger cities could support a metalsmith who worked in brass, iron and silver. In Boston, New York and Philadelphia, metalsmiths made andirons, buttons and just a bit of jewelry. The industry gradually centralized in Providence, Rhode Island for a number of contributing reasons.

Ships' captains and traders of Rhode Island accumulated silver coins through their rum-slaves-molasses routes. To enable identification of their own silver, merchants had the coins fashioned into silver objects such as tea pots, trays, porringers, tankards and so forth with their initials engraved upon them. By the late eighteenth century, a small group of silversmiths were working in Providence.

In 1784, Seril Dodge was one of six silversmiths here who made plate and jewelry. In 1793, he advertised gold jewelry, silver spoons, silver plated shoe buckles and knee buckles, cyphered and brilliant stone buttons, and plated spurs. In the same advertisment, he offered to buy gold, silver, copper and brass. [Alfred M. Weisberg, *Why Providence?*, Technic, Inc., Providence, R.I., 1988, p.2.] The plated silver mentioned in his advertisment was probably heat-fused silver on copper, similar to what was called *Sheffield plate* in England.

In the early nineteenth century, silversmiths made silver shoe and knee buckes and silver buttons for the fashionably elite. While New England ladies then were not noted for wearing jewelry, they did adorn themselves with fancy buttons that were removed before a garment was laundered.

By 1825, women in America began to wear small, delicate filigree pins and clasps. Before 1840, practically no diamonds were imported into the United States, but between 1840 and 1850, the imports of diamonds grew ten-fold. [*Providence*, p.6.] In 1850, American manufacturing of jewelry, including silver styles, was encouraged by a high tariff imposed on foreign jewelry. Thereafter, the manufacturing jewelry industry in Providence grew rapidly.

By the 1870s, emblematic jewelry and secret society charms became a major industry in Providence in silver as well as gold. Periodic economic recessions in the nineteenth century caused temporary set-backs for the industry, but after each set-back the industry grew stronger.

Prospecting for silver in the late nineteenth century grew economically more attractive as there was an increased demand for silver items internationally. The roaring industrial revolution provided so many improvements in the manufacturing potentials for silver, that more and more companies joined the output of products. Therefore, silver jewelry became so plentiful, and inexpensive, that the growing middle classes could enjoy the pleasure of adornment as even their affluent ancestors could not have dreamed.

The development of silver jewelry designs in the twentieth century followed the general art trends through the decades. Abundant volume of designs for an eager population were sold through mail order catalogs, special departments of large stores, and artist-craftsmen. Therefore, they display a wide variety of craftsmanship and amount of machine-age technology. The jewelry is a wonderful reflection of the people who designed, made and owned it. Today, it is particularly appreciated for its diversity.

Silver Techniques

Filigree

Ornamentation of fine wire work is known as *filigree*. Examples of fine filigree work originate in the Orient, India, and the Mediterranean rim. The thin wires are either soldered to a metal base plate or freestanding. Ancient filigree techniques were revived in the nineteenth century which influenced the styles found in the twentieth century.

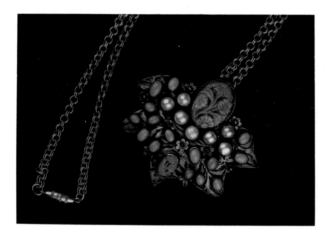

Silver filigree pendant washed with gold and set with glass coral and pearl.

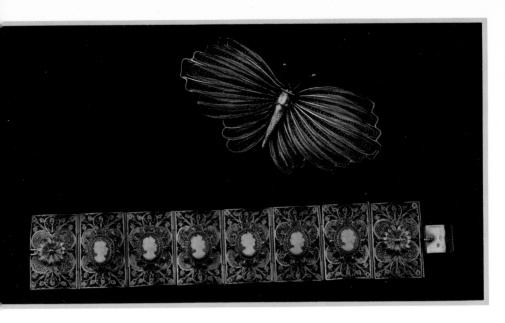

Silver filigree butterfly brooch, unsigned. Bracelet of 800 German silver filigree links set with cameos.

Silver filigree shaped as a large flower with intricately worked petals and leaves, marked "Made in Mexico."

Bracelet of square filigree links set with enameled panels, marked "Portugal;" sterling silver bow brooch with filigree pendant and pink facet-cut stone, marked "GY;" necklace of silver with large filigree pendant set with turquoise and supporting silver chain fringe, marked "J.S.;" link bracelet of filigree panels with enameled embellishment, unmarked.

Finely detailed scatter pins of silver filigree designed as moths and complex geometric shapes.

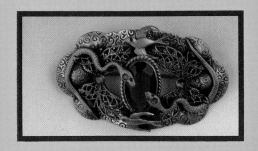

Brooch of gilded silver filigree and stamped elements set with colored glass stones, c. 1920.

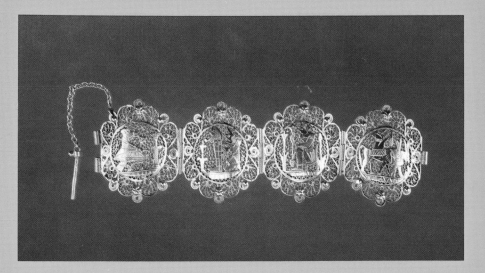

Egyptian motifs with engraved details are mounted on fine silver filigree panels for this link bracelet, c. 1940.

Carved ivory figures of Chinese men are mounted on silver filigree panels for this finger ring and pair of earrings, c. 1940.

Openwork

Pierced metalwork to form a design is known as *openwork*. Sometimes used in conjunction with filigree, it can also be used independently and with further engraved or chased designs on the flat surfaces. Bohemian metalworkers of the early twentieth century were particularly adept at openwork which is displayed in many jewelry articles, especially those set with glass jewels.

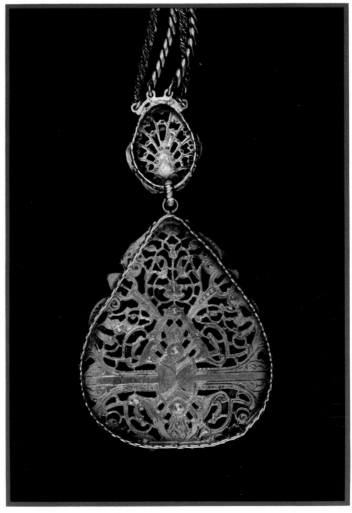

Above and opposite:
Two pair of earrings and pendant necklace with silver openwork technique decoration and set with colored glass rhinestones, probably from Czechoslovakia, c. 1930.

The silver filigree panels of the brooch and pendant necklace
are each finely detailed. The pendant has a very good quality
glass cabochon with asterism and small enameled accents, c.
1930. Contrasting the filigree are good examples of openwork
detailing in the bead and silver chain necklace and the drop
earrings, both set with blue glass balls. The bangle bracelet,
also set with blue glass stones, has a stamped design on the
solid silver rim, c. 1935.

Silver filigree supports the faux pearls and colored rhinestones
on this splendid pendant brooch, c. 1940.

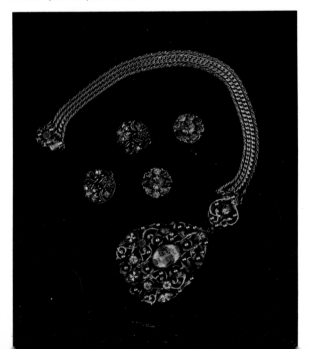

Sterling silver openwork disc brooch marked "ILG" with engraved details, probably English, c. 1930.

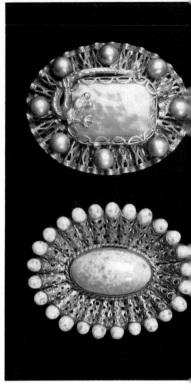

Two silver openwork brooches set with faux turquoise, c. 1930. Dennis Cogdell.

Necklace of silver openwork panels set with purple rhinestones and accented with green enamel, c. 1930.

Link bracelet of openwork panels in Symmetalic silver and golc wash, c. 1940.

Oriental silver openwork links set with rhinestones and joined
to form a belt, c. 1925.

Matching link and pendant necklace and flexible bracelet of
openwork panels set with cabochon rhinestones, c. 1940.

Repoussé

Raised designs which are produced by hammering or punching the silver are known as *repoussé*. Fine detail can be achieved to produce very elaborated ornamentation. The technique is also known as *embossing*. Further details can be added with chasing and engraving to produce a very deep design.

Oriental silver link bracelet of repoussé decoration and set with three cabochons of lapis lazuli marked "China," c. 1940.

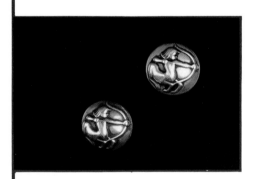

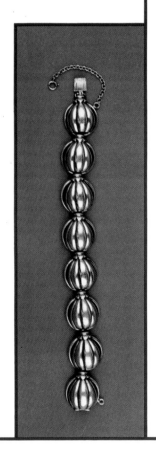

Sterling silver repoussé, button style earrings with a representation of the Zodiac sign for Sagittarius (November 22 to December 22) as a Centaur with a bow and arrow, designed by Joseff of Hollywood as part of a line of jewelry featuring the Zodiac, c. 1945.

Sterling silver melon-shaped links form a bracelet by Napier, c. 1960.

Inlay

The ornamentation of the surface of an object with shaped pieces of a different material is known as *inlay*. Often the resulting surface is filled and polished level. In the case of jewelry, the inlay is generally another metal, stone, ivory, shell or glass.

Turquoise chips are inlayed in a matrix with silver backing in this set of bangle bracelet, earrings and two brooches marked "India," c. 1940.

Jewelry Designs

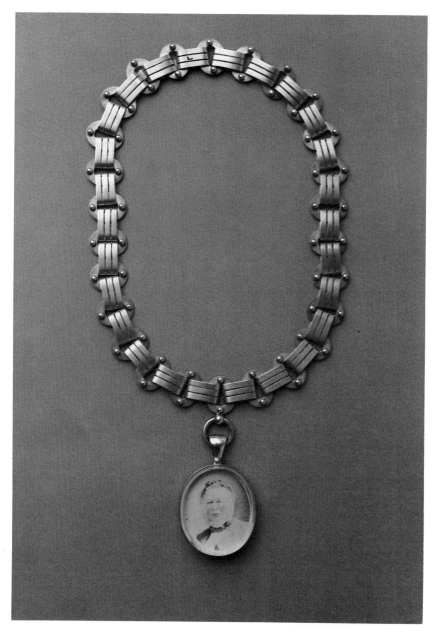

Silver link chain necklace and pendant locket enclosing two photographs, English, c. 1880. Maureen McEvoy

Old World Classics

Hair comb and ornament of sterling silver openwork set with cushion shaped diamonds, English, c. 1885.

Silver drop earrings set with iron pyrites, c. 1890. Harvey & Gore.

Sterling silver and leaves of ivory form three folding tablets from the late ninteenth century. At the left, the six rectangular interior leaves are marked Monday through Saturday, c. 1840. The center tablet with repoussé scrolls has seven ivory leaves, a silver chain, and an attached mechanical pencil, c. 1900. The rococo tablet has six conforming leaves, c. 1870.

Sterling silver trefoil brooch with openwork pendant, c. 1900. Pair of sterling silver clips joined with a silver link chain as a cape fastener, c. 1900.

Chatelaine of sterling silver marked "A. Barrett & Sons, 63 & 64
Piccadilly, London" which includes a pin cushion, shoe button
hook, vinagrette, needle holder, locket, watch key and whistle,
c. 1900.

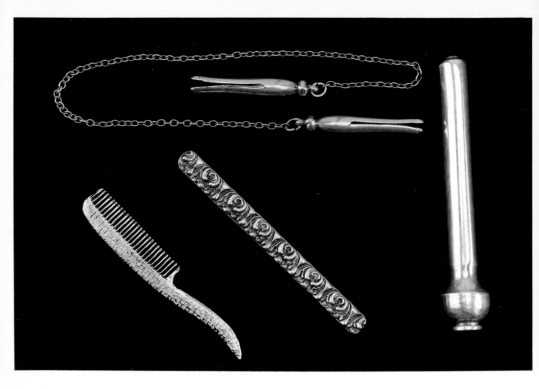

Small sterling silver dresser utensils were popular accessories at the turn of the century. Here we see a plain needle case, letter opener, mustache comb, and cape chain with clips. J. Fleischmann.

Sterling silver lorgnette with repoussé case and wrist chain, c. 1900. Sandy DeMaio Antiques.

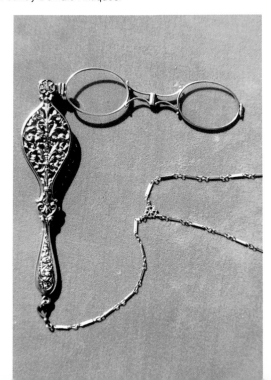

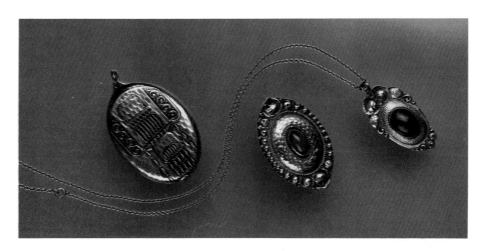

Three German repoussé ornaments, c. 1910: a locket, a
brooch of "800" silver set with cabochon carnelian, and a
pendant set with lapis lazuli. Carole A. Berk, Ltd.

Repoussé silver heart locket marked "F&B" in a pennant for
the Foster & Bailey Co. of Providence, R. I., c. 1890. Small silver
heart locket with twisted wire and green turquoise ornaments.
Child's silver rattle with strap hanger. Repoussé silver whistle
with ring hanger.

Small sentimental brooches of silver with naturalistic images: bar pin with enameled owls in fine detail; round frame with hummingbird painted under glass; round frame with lady by a window painted under glass; oval frame with two doves picked out in gold and under glass; small round sterling silver vase with leaf decoration; and a tall urn of sterling silver marked by Monet, c. 1940.

Scottish silver brooch of deep repoussé thistle pattern around a faceted quartz stone, c. 1920. Michael Greenberg.

English sterling silver postage stamp case of envelope shape made in Birmingham.

Set of silver buttons decorated in repoussé to represent the Zodiac sign for Pisces (February 19 to March 21) which is two fish. The buttons are finished with silver wire loops in the backs, c. 1915.

Silver cherub brooches from the 1920s hover protectively over Chinese silver fish, also mounted as brooches.

Art Nouveau brooch of sterling silver with a particularly graceful design incorporating a peacock and idealized woman's profile. Lyn Trusdell.

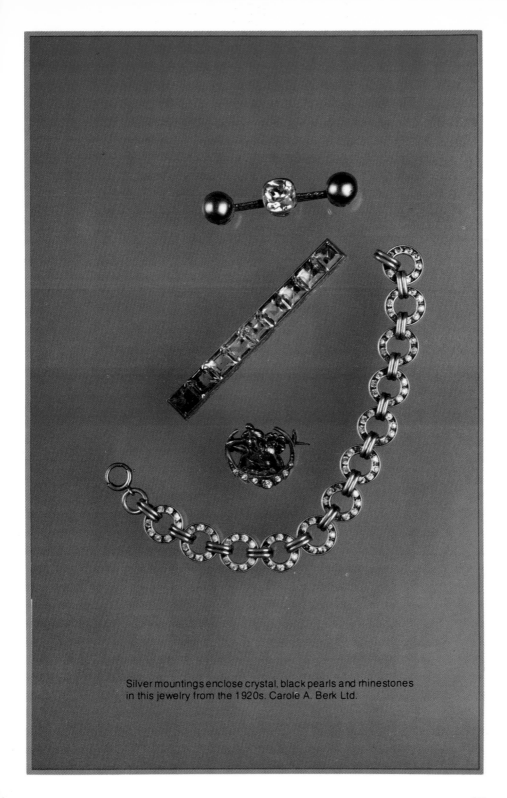

Silver mountings enclose crystal, black pearls and rhinestones in this jewelry from the 1920s. Carole A. Berk Ltd.

The firm of Theodor Fahrner in Pforzheim, Germany created these pendants and brooches of silver. From top clockwise: pendant with ivory parrot carving, lapis lazuli cabochons and marcasite, c.1920; pendant with amazonite, lapis lazuli and marcasite, c. 1926-30; brooch with coral and marcasite, c. 1925; and brooch with silver leaves and chrysoprases, c. 1910-14.

Brooch of silver set with marcasites and onyx from the firm of Theodor Fahrner, c. 1930. Linda Morgan.

Brooch of silver with amethyst drops from the firm of Theodor Fahrner, c. 1908.

Link bracelet of silver with marcasites from the Theodor Fahrner firm, c. 1925. M. Klein.

Silver and rhinestones in a figural brooch design with plenty of
personality from the 1950s. Jackie Fleischman.

Modern Inspiration

Fine sterling silver bead necklace of five strands with beautifully
engraved keepers, c. 1928. M. Karasik.

Men's silver finger rings from the 1930s, from the top clockwise: carved jade with three bars of jet on each side; Gold band with smaller silver overlay; square top with four bars of silver overlay, signed "J. Després"; and two panther heads, signed "Delon". M. Klein.

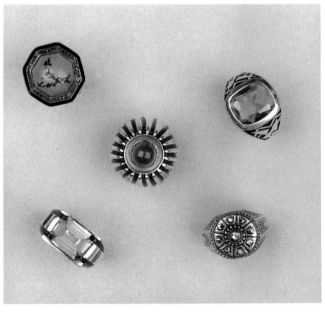

French silver rings from the 1930s set, from top clockwise, with a rose-cut diamond and semi-precious stones: aquamarine, turquoise, amethyst, and carnelian. M. Klein.

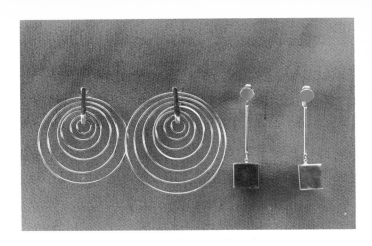

Two pair of silver dangling earrings of strong geometric design, c. 1928. J. Fleischmann.

Sterling silver cuff bracelets and a pair of dangling earrings from the 1930s in sleek, direct designs.

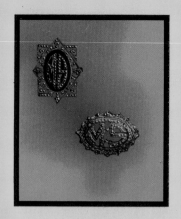

Personalized brooches made with silver and marcasites in the initials of the original owner by Schreiner Jewels of New York in the 1930s.

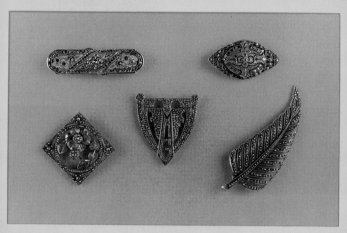

Five silver brooches set with marcasites, c. 1930. M. Klein

Bow brooch of silver with marcasites, c. 1925-30. Linda Morgan.

Satyr brooch/pendant of silver set with marcasites.

From the 1930s, silver jewelry set with marcasites: floral brooch; pendant of crystal in a frame and with floral application; safety-pin brooch; pendant of crystal in a hexagonal frame with geometric application; and a German necklace with silver link chain and pendant set with carnelians. Carol A. Berk, Ltd.

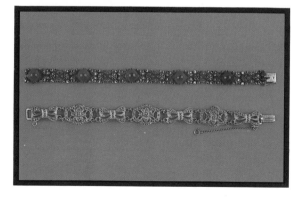

Link bracelet of German 800 silver set with marcasites and green cabochons. Sterling silver openwork bracelet of bow- and plaque-shaped links. M. Klein.

Three pair of silver openwork earrings set with marcasites, c. 1930. M. Klein.

Sterling silver jewelry from the 1930s set with marcasites and semi-precious stones, unmarked. Carole A. Berk, Ltd.

Silver brooches and paired clips set with marcasites and coral, c. 1935. Fior

Lovely link necklace and earrings of silver set with marcasites, c. 1935. Malvina Solomon.

Two fine silver link
necklaces set with
marcasites, c. 1935.
Malvina Solomon.

Intricate silver drop earrings set with marcasites, c. 1935.

Marcasites and amethysts are joined in a delicate silver linked design for this spectacular necklace and drop earrings. Malvina Solomon.

Earrings from the 1930s of silver and marcasites with green stones and onyx drops. Malvina Solomon.

Imaginative earring designs from the 1930s rendered in silver and marcasites. Malvina Solomon.

Pendant necklace and drop earrings of silver and jet set with marcasites.

A floral basket brooch and pairs of earrings constructed from silver with colored stones and marcasite accents, c. 1940. Fior.

Geometric designs beautifully executed in French silver earrings from the 1930s with enamel, colored stones and marcasites. M. Klein.

Sterling silver earrings from the 1930s with hematite, freshwater pearls and marcasites. Bizarre Bazaar.

Rings on her fingers in assorted designs from the 1930s with silver, marcasites and colored stones. The variations make the search for different forms a fascinating preoccupation. Fior.

Spanish-American

Hinged bracelets of silver from Mexico, c. 1945; above, with
concha shell inlay and a wonderfully strong swirl design
marked ALPAGA; below, with amethyst balls and masks.

Mexican sterling silver brooches and earrings that feature *concha* shell inlay, c. 1945.

Mexican silver brooches and a link bracelet featuring *concha* shell inlay, c. 1940. Frances Cronin.

Earrings and brooches with *concha* shell inlaid in silver, Mexican, c. 1940s. Frances Cronin.

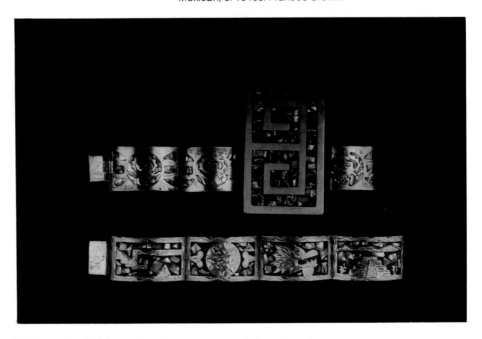

Buckle and two link bracelets of *concha* shell and silver, the lower bracelet marked "ARL," Mexican, c. 1945.

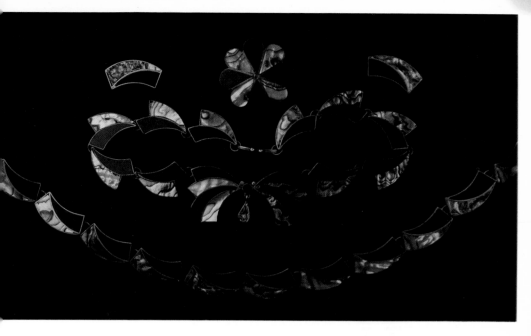

Set of Mexican silver jewelry featuring onyx and *concha* shell inlay, c. 1945.

Bangle bracelet of silver loop design and *concha* shell inlay, c. 1940. Frances Cronin.

Matching set of silver link jewelry from Taxco, Mexico, c. 1945.

Set of silver jewelry marked "ELNA, Mexico," c. 1945.

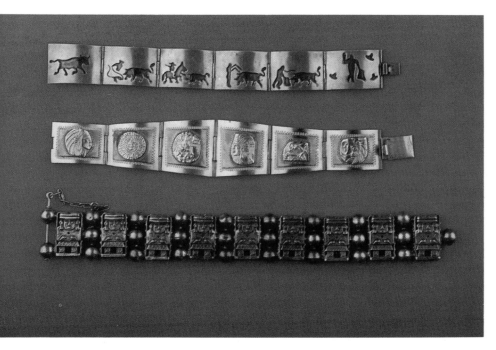

Three Mexican silver link bracelets with designs derived from
Mexico's rich history, c. 1945.

Turquoise chips are inlaid and polished to a smooth surface in this jewelry that is marked "Hand made guaranteed sterling 925 Guad Mex RMS."

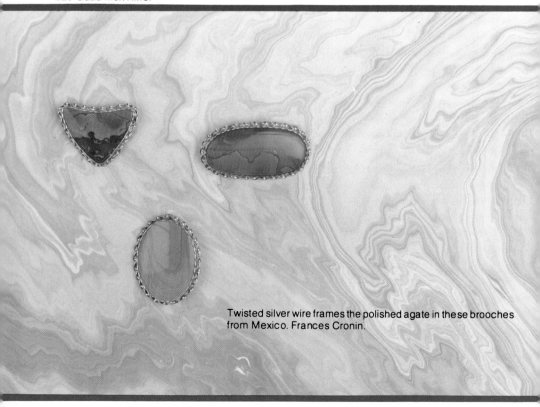

Twisted silver wire frames the polished agate in these brooches from Mexico. Frances Cronin.

This Mexican jewelry features stone ornaments as intergral parts of the designs.

The turbaned head brooch of silver and lavulite displays its pre-Columbian design source in the strong facial features and exaggerated proportions of the turban and ear pendants. The geometric link bracelet is marked "J.S. Taxco, Mexico." E. & J. Rothstein Antiques.

Link bracelet with onyx and silver ball ornaments marked "Mexico." The pendant is engraved with a pre-Columbian inspired geometric design and treated to achieve a black surface. The link bracelet with obsidian mask is marked "ALOA."

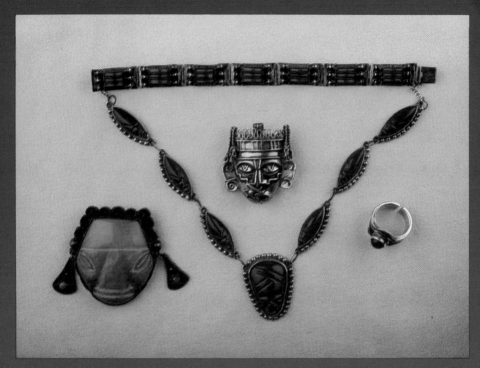

Carved green stones are featured in this group of Mexican jewelry from the 1940s with silver mountings. The silver mask pendant in the center has a particularly geometric stylized design.

Obsidian carved masks are framed with silver in this ring and earrings marked "Mexico."

Mexican sterling silver earclips and brooches in modern designs from the 1950s. Frances Cronin.

A set of Mexican copper and silver earclips and brooch, c. 1950. Frances Cronin.

Silver earclips with green and blue enamel body by Salvador Teran, Mexico, c. 1955. Christie's, London.

Mexican silver cuff bracelet signed "Maricela", the shop of Ysidro Garcia Pina of Taxco, with openwork and applied decoration, c. 1950. Rope braid silver cuff bracelet by Hector Aguilar of Taxco, c. 1940. Lynn Trusdell.

Brooches of silver floral design set with green cabochon stones, both from Taxco, Mexico, c. 1945.

Turquoise centers ornament the silver flowerheads of this matching necklace and bracelet marked "Taxco, 980," c. 1945.

Opposite:
Pin and earrings of sterling silver in floral bud design marked "Taxco, 940." Pin designed as a pair of flowers and marked "NOE" in a trefoil, c. 1950.

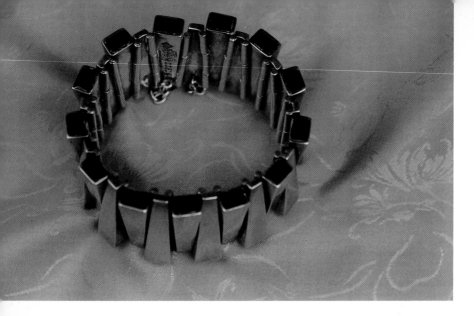

Silver trapezoids are placed on edge to create this bracelet with black glass set into the ends, marked "Hecho en Mexico # ZZ514." M. Klein.

Necklace and earclips of hollow silver scrolls marked "Tu.N1 Mexico 925."

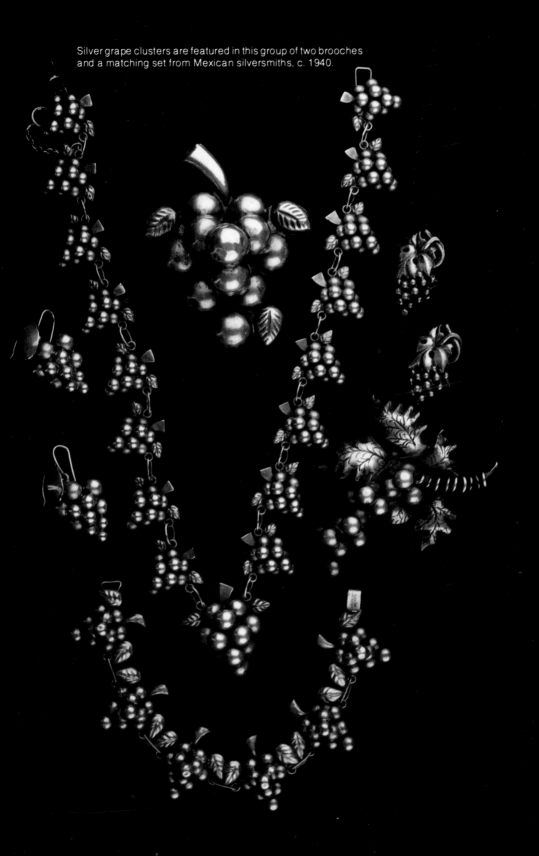

Silver grape clusters are featured in this group of two brooches and a matching set from Mexican silversmiths, c. 1940.

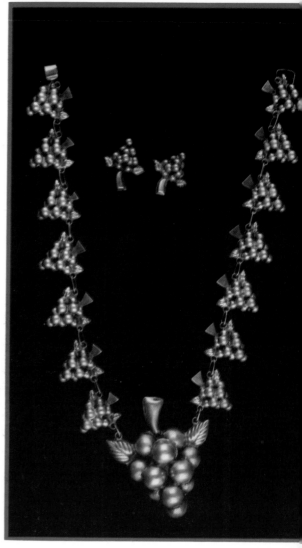

A cluster of grapes motif is repeated in this silver necklace and earclips set from Mexico, c. 1950.

Brooch of black and brown enamel on silver in abstract geometric design, Mexican. Ear drops of silver with abstracted design, Mexican. M. Klein.

Six Peruvian silver link bracelets with strong designs representing animals and figures in traditional and ceremonial dress. c. 1940s.

World In Conflict

Brooch and earclips of candelabra design in silver with glass pearl drops, c. 1940. Cobra & Bellamy.

These necklaces from the 1940s represent two competing styles: on the left, the use of glass beads and faceted rhinestones set in silver follows the traditional concept of glittering jewels. On the right, the necklace design has grown from the modern, streamlined, abstracted style. Both were probably made in Germany. Fior.

The intricate silver chain bracelet is probably of German manufacture, although it is unmarked. The charm bracelet is marked "800" silver and encloses small coral, turquoise and carnelian cabochons, c. 1940.

Enameled silver pansy brooch and earclips from the 1940s.

Faceted rhinestones are set in beautifully worked silver settings for this group from the 1940s, only the necklace is marked "Jerusalem silver."

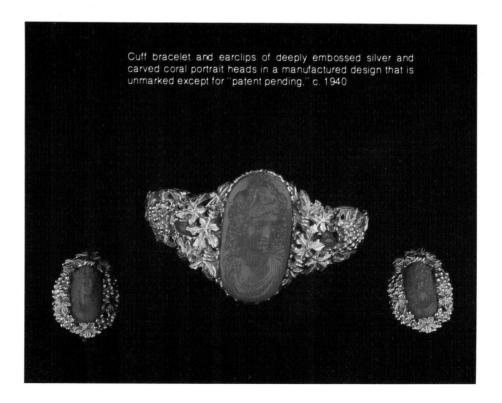

Cuff bracelet and earclips of deeply embossed silver and carved coral portrait heads in a manufactured design that is unmarked except for "patent pending." c. 1940

Personal monograms became popular mementos in the 1940s and these silver examples demonstrate diversity in styles from geometric to ornately scrolled. Frances Cronin.

Silver figural pins from the 1940s, unmarked.

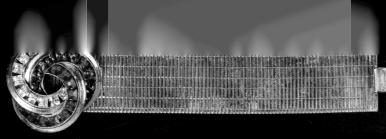

A wonderful silver mesh bracelet and matching brooch set with rhinestones could have been made for the French or American market in the 1940s. It is not signed. Norman Crider Antiques.

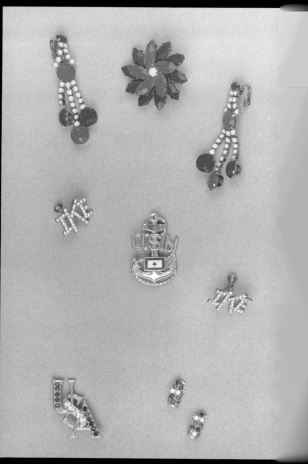

Sterling silver brooch in rhinestones and blue enamel of the United States flag, c. 1940.

Brooch and matching earclips set with opaque colored gla stones. The "IKE" earrings were worn to show support Dwight Eisenhower, nicknamed "Ike," when he w Commander of Allied Troops in the Second World War, or wh he was a candidate for the presidency of the United States 1953 or 1957. The "USN" pin is a jewelry replica of a Unit States Navy insignia. Frances Cronin.

Silver settings washed in gold and set with red, white and blue rhinestones. The flower spray brooch is marked "Reinad." The bug has enameled wings which tremble on tiny springs. Norman Crider Antiques.

The American Eagle and the Dove of Peace are popular American patriotic symbols proudly worn and these silver and gold washed brooches are fine examples of the variety that was made in the 1940s. Norman Crider Antiques.

The silver watch bracelet and watch ring were designed by
Torun Bülow-Hübe for Georg Jensen, Denmark, c. 1960.
Tadema Gallery.

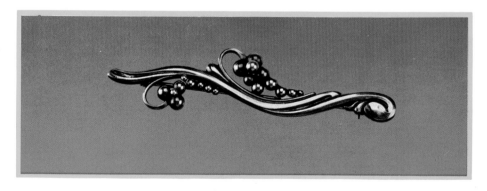

Lovely flowing lines comprise this sterling silver bar pin by
Georg Jensen, c. 1950.

The yellow enamel on silver necklace of baby chicks links is marked "Denmark," c. 1940. The embossed oval brooch, match holder and child's rattel marked "Webster" all date from the mid-century era.

Sterling and black enamel brooch and earclips marked "A.J. Denmark." Carole A. Berk Ltd.

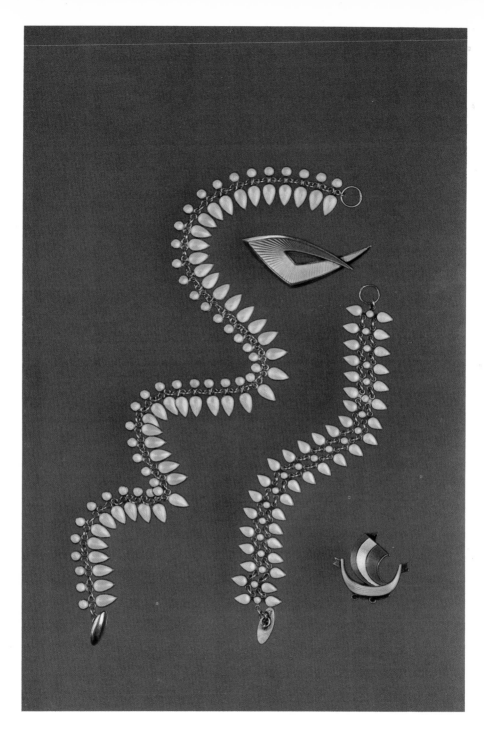

The fringe necklace and bracelet of enameled sterling silver
links is marked "V D Denmark." The abstract and Viking ship
enameled sterling silver brooches are both marked "Norway."

This group of enameled sterling silver link necklace and three brooches was made by David Andersen of Norway. Carole A. Berk, Ltd.

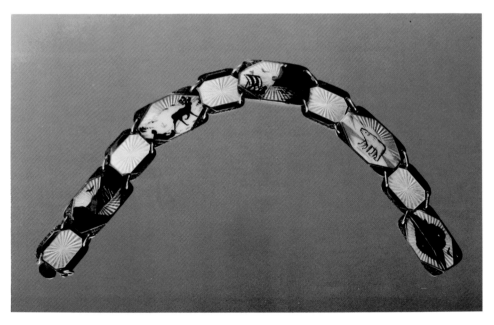

Link bracelet of enamel on silver with Arctic images carefully delineated, c. 1950.

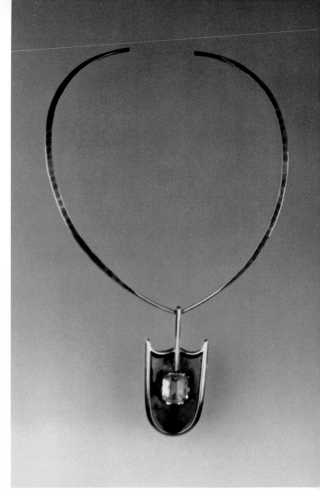

Sterling silver pendant with blue
enamel and aquamarine by
David Andersen of Norway
supported by a sculpted neck
wire. Carole A. Berk, Ltd.

Sterling silver brooches of
Scandinavian origin, c. 1940:
top marked "Viking Craft;"
center marked "Danecraft;"
bottom not marked. Carole A.
Berk, Ltd.

An enameled sterling silver brooch by Balle of Norway rests above another enameled silver brooch by Thune of Norway, both made c. 1960. Carole A. Berk, Ltd.

David Andersen of Norway made this group of technically excellent enameled jewelry in abstract and regular geometric designs. Carole A. Berk, Ltd.

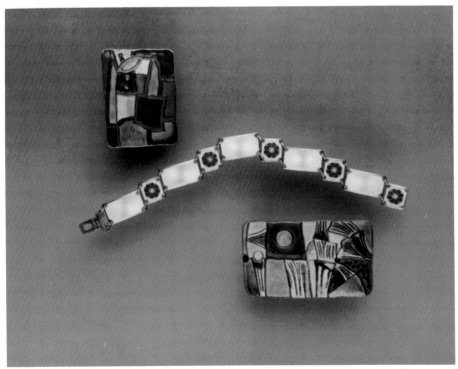

Mid-Century Realism

Floral brooches became enormously popular in the 1950s as many new designers competed for the growing market for costume jewelry. These sterling silver and rhinestone examples are not marked by a maker.

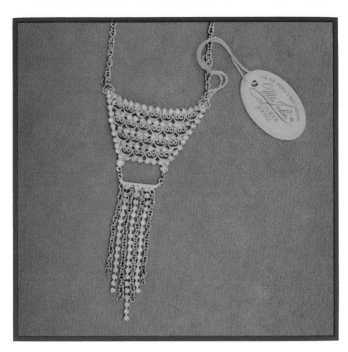

Silver chain and rhinestones are combined in this necklace that was sold by "Mr. John Couturier Jewels," c. 1955. B. Hopper.

Intricate silver frames surround onyx on this pair of earclips by Peruzzi of Florence, c. 1952. B. Hopper.

Delicate floral designs, more than any other motif, characterize the jewelry of the optimistic 1950s. These silver brooches show a cross section of the styles made, and none are marked by their maker. Frances Cronin.

Detailed, hand-constructed designs with many assembled elements characterize the sterling silver Hobé jewelry from the 1940s. These brooches and link bracelet are exquisitely crafted. E. & J. Rothstein Antiques.

Magnificent sterling silver brooches of large size and set with faceted rhinestones were created by Hobé in the 1940s. Carole A. Berk, Ltd.

Sterling silver brooches in the 1950s were generally designed with floral motifs, as are these intricated examples by Hobé of New York. Carole A. Berk, Ltd.

Individually cut-out silver flowers and leaves surround colored rhinestones on the bracelet and pendant by Hobé. The reverse of the jewelry shows an intricate wirework backing to which all the front pieces are attached. Skilled hand construction was required to build each piece individually.

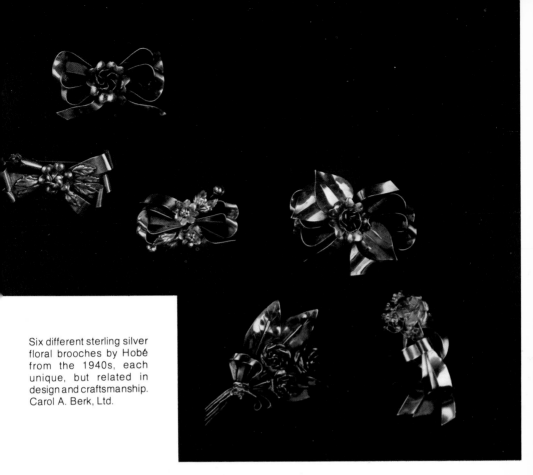

Six different sterling silver floral brooches by Hobé from the 1940s, each unique, but related in design and craftsmanship. Carol A. Berk, Ltd.

14 kt gold plated elements are combined with sterling silver and colored rhinestones on these pieces by Hobé from the 1940s.

Jewelry designer Guglielmo Cini was trained as young man in Florence, Italy before immigrating to the United States in 1922. He established a workshop in Boston where he worked until 1957 when he relocated to Laguna Beach, California. His designs in sterling and gold plated silver echo a rich European tradition and responded to the American market particularly. Design catalogs of 1941 and 1963 display many of his successful silver jewelry items.

"A large spray pin adapted from an old French design of flower and leaf forms with delicate pendant lily of the valley blossoms" [G. Cini's catalog of 1941, item #2] with matching earrings and ring. On the right, a large sterling silver bouquet of rambling roses [G. Cini's catalog of 1963, p. 64.] E. & J. Rothstein Antiques.

Images of classical Italian persona are beautifully interpreted
with great deatil in this sterling silver jewelry by G. Cini, c. 1963.
E. & J. Rothstein Antiques.

Lacy openwork and repousse scrolls are combined with smooth balls for this Baroque design sterling silver set of jewelry by G. Cini, c. 1963.

Wildflowers and withering leaves are authentically depicted in these floral designs in sterling silver by G. Cini, c. 1941 to 1963. E. & J. Rothstein Antiques.

Opposite:
Progressively more frequently in the decades of the 1950s and 1960s, G. Cini included faceteted colored rhinestones in his compositions. These brooches of sterling silver span the period from 1941 to 1963. E. & J. Rothstein Antiques.

A happy little clown was just made to add amusement to life, and he does! This sterling silver brooch was made by G. Cini about 1960. E. & J. Rothstein Antiques.

Butterflies are another naturalistic subject G. Cini used for his jewelry designs. The large butterfly brooch appears in the 1941 catalog, and the smaller brooches and earclips appear in the 1963 catalog. E. & J. Rothstein Antiques.

One of nature's most prized flowers, the orchid inspired the design for this set of sterling silver jewelry by G. Cini, c. 1960. E. & J. Rothstein Antiques.

Old World tradition is reflected in this crown and shield design by G. Cini for the sterling silver matching set, c. 1963. E. & J. Rothstein Antiques.

Opposite:
G. Cini produced these delicate designs for rings, brooches and earclips in sterling silver c. 1963. E. & J. Rothstein Antiques.

The belt and bracelets are sensational compositions of ornate
design and intricate workmanship produced by G. Cini, c. 1963.
E. & J. Rothstein Antiques.

Opposite:
To proclaim joy for Allied victory in World War II, G. Cini made
this (Victory) and the American eagle brooch available, c.
1945. His ornate key brooch and turtle box in sterling silver
were made c. 1941. E. & J. Rothstein Antiques.

G. Cini transformaed sterling silver into individual flower heads
and a buckeye leaf and pod through his designs for these
sterling silver brooches, c. 1963. E. & J. Rothstein Antiques.

A silver plated plaque with applied *fleur de lis* and shading made, c. 1940, by Francisco Rebajes of New York.

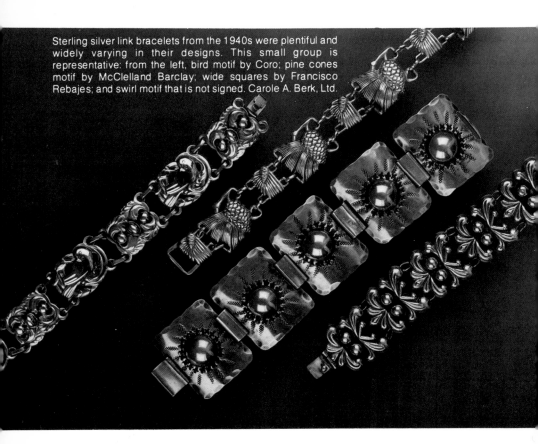

Sterling silver link bracelets from the 1940s were plentiful and widely varying in their designs. This small group is representative: from the left, bird motif by Coro; pine cones motif by McClelland Barclay; wide squares by Francisco Rebajes; and swirl motif that is not signed. Carole A. Berk, Ltd.

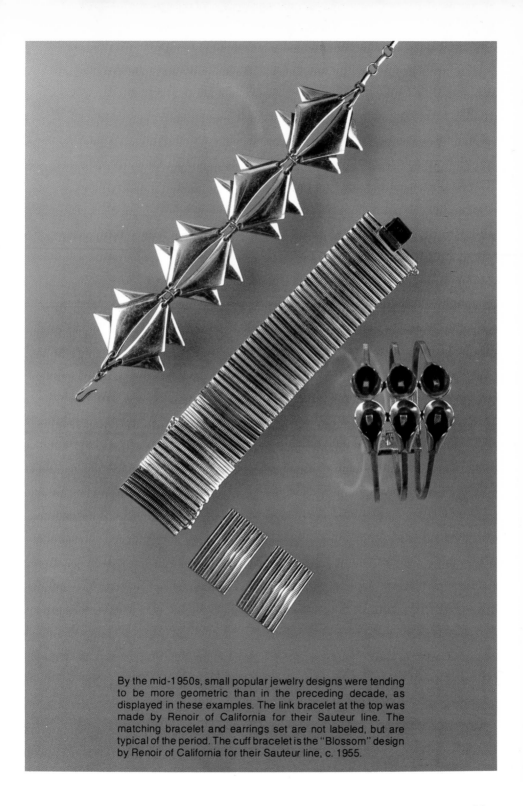

By the mid-1950s, small popular jewelry designs were tending to be more geometric than in the preceding decade, as displayed in these examples. The link bracelet at the top was made by Renoir of California for their Sauteur line. The matching bracelet and earrings set are not labeled, but are typical of the period. The cuff bracelet is the "Blossom" design by Renoir of California for their Sauteur line, c. 1955.

Atomic Age

Figural pins abounded in the 1960s with designs more simplified than previously. These sterling silver and plated silver examples of lively fish, stars, bugs and birds are a small sampling of the delightful diversity to be found. Frances Cronin.

95

Animal themes also captured the imaginations for figural pin
designers in the 1960s. These designs are generally not as
intricate as the styles of the earlier decades. The pins shown
here are not marked. Frances Cronin.

Horse enthusiasts always have a good selection of silver
jewelry to wear. **Lynn Trusdell.**

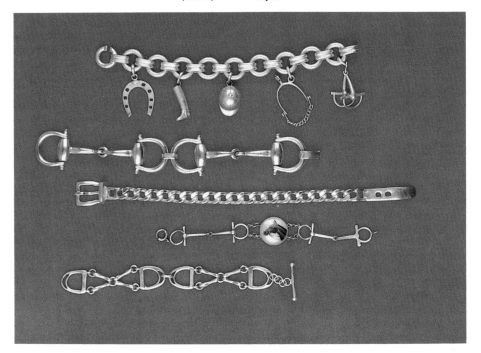

A Napier link bracelet of silver is attractively made, but when the pendant beads and matching earclips are added, the result becomes sensational. During the 1960s, such surprises in design were frequently attempted. Muriel Karasik.

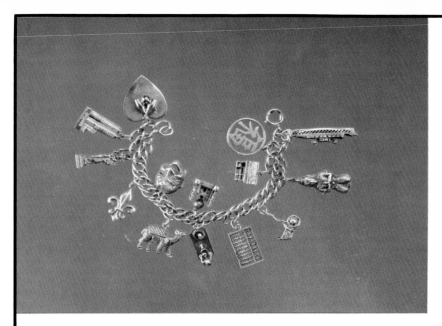

Charm bracelets were a mainstay in a lady's jewel box for two generations. From the 1940s through the 1960s, millions of small representative charms were created. Owners assembled their bracelets as keepsakes to remember friends, places, hobbies, events-anything sentimental and personally important. Frances Cronin.

These children's bracelets have a sweet innocence in their designs. The gold washed silver bangle spells out nursery rhymes. The Mexican silver bangle has cut-out voids in the forms of bull fighters. And the charm bracelet is only for dog owners. These must have made their owners very happy.

99

A sterling silver oak leaf clip with wooden acorns is signed "Bill Ilfield." The silver acorn earrings are not marked.

A simply made bird brooch of lively design marked "Sterling-craft by Coro" hovers over a Napier flower brooch of silver, c. 1960. Carole A. Berk, Ltd.

A silver dogwood brooch with moonstones and a petaled flower with green glass rhinestones both marked "Coro Made in Mexico."

The round brooches of uncomplicated design are by Napier and the triangular brooch of loops is by Monet, c. 1950. Carole A. Berk, Ltd.

Sterling scrolls and flowers set with rhinestones from the 1960s. The brooch with a green stone is marked "Van."

A silver wire bracelet by Napier, c. 1955. Carole A. Berk, Ltd.

Sterling floral brooch set with a blue cabochon by Coro.

A silver link bracelet by Kramer of New York in a very simple design from the 1960s and an unmarked necklace of gold plated silver and real nut beads from the 1960s. Fior.

Square silver beads are linked to form a long chain on this
necklace and the earrings are gold plated silver flower heads.
Both bear the label of Monet and date from the 1960s. B.
Hopper

Whiting and Davis made these bracelets and earclips with
silver repousse and mesh in the 1960s. B. Hopper.

Fine silver mesh and openwork present the decoration of this
jewelry by Napier from the 1960s. B. Hopper.

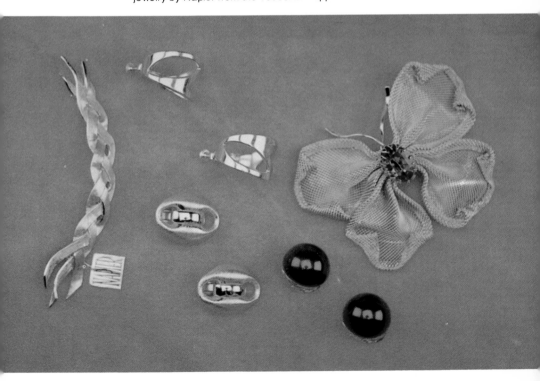

Sheer geometry in a domed silver brooch without markings, straight out of the 1960s.

Monet sterling silver drop earclips with turquoise and a link bracelet, c. 1965.

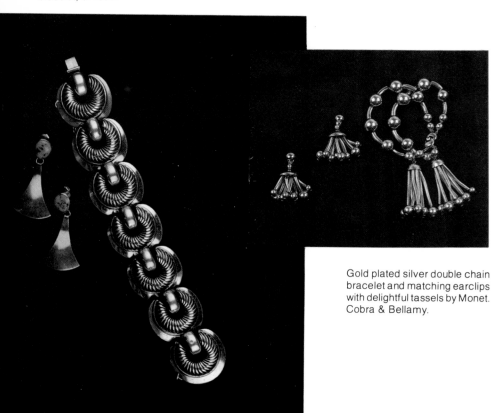

Gold plated silver double chain bracelet and matching earclips with delightful tassels by Monet. Cobra & Bellamy.

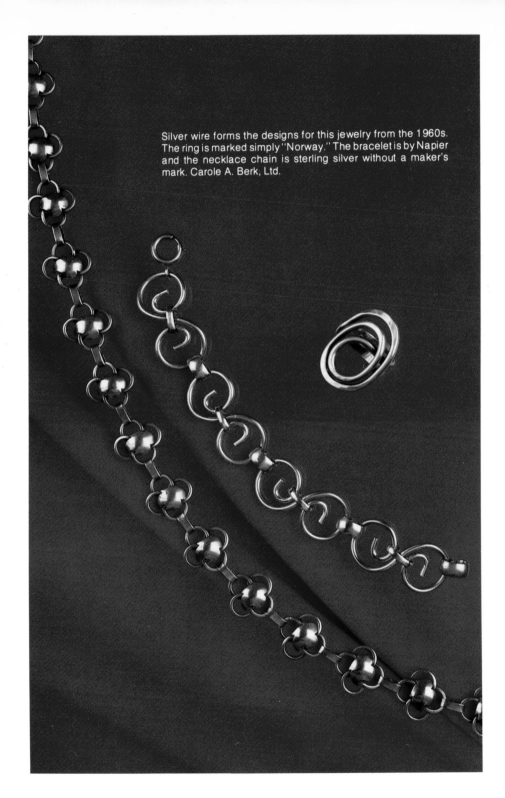

Silver wire forms the designs for this jewelry from the 1960s. The ring is marked simply "Norway." The bracelet is by Napier and the necklace chain is sterling silver without a maker's mark. Carole A. Berk, Ltd.

Native American

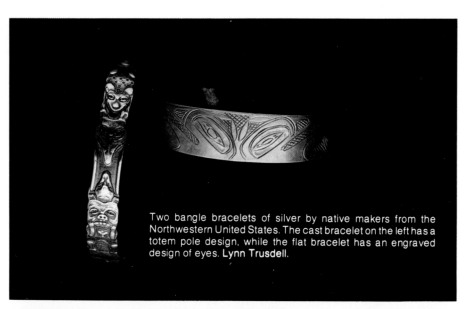

Two bangle bracelets of silver by native makers from the Northwestern United States. The cast bracelet on the left has a totem pole design, while the flat bracelet has an engraved design of eyes. **Lynn Trusdell.**

Five fascinating designs for cuff bracelets of engraved silver by native makers from the Northwestern United States. **Lynn Trusdell.**

Southwest American Indians, probably from the Navajo tribe, made these superb silver cuff bracelets with stamped and repousse designs in the first half of the twentieth century. Lynn Trusdell.

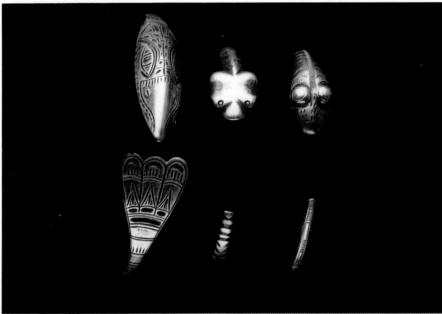

Three snake-style silver bracelets are shown. The largest was made by natives from the Northwestern United States, while the two smaller bracelets were made by Navajo Indians of the American Southwest. They make a wonderful comparison of the two different native styles. **Lynn Trusdell.**

This wonderful group of silver bracelets by Navajo Indians of the American Southwest demonstrate the diversity of techniques in which the silversmiths here are proficient. Twisted wire, stamping, repousse, engraving and shadowbox styles are all presented. **Lynn Trusdell**.

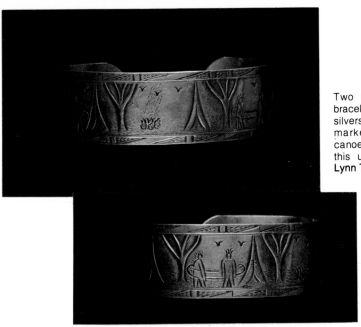

Two views of a silver bracelet made by a Navajo silversmith for the tourist market. Teepees and canoes are featured on this unmarked bracelet. **Lynn Trusdell.**

Two fine Navajo silver bracelets, one bearing the mark of the trade association begun in 1938, reading "U. S. Navajo." **Lynn Trusdell.**

Navajo-made necklaces of hand-constructed silver beads and links, probably from the 1930s.

These bracelets with Indian head, arrow, and thunderbird designs were made by Navajo silversmiths primarily for the tourist trade in the 1940s. Lynn Trusdell.

Wide silver cuff bracelets of this type would be worn by Navajo
men and women alike. These probably date from the 1930s
through the 1950s. **Lynn Trusdell.**

A fine hair comb of cut, stamped and raised silver made by a
Hopi silversmith from Arizona.

This very large silver bracelet of cut, stamped and wire pieces supports a turquoise stone from the Morenci mine. B. Hopper.

Contemporary silver belts of the concho tradition include such modern contrivances as a linked style and ranger type buckles. Palms Trading Company.

This large silver wirework cuff bracelet by Navajo silversmith Art Tafoya supports a turquoise stone from the Blue Diamond mine. B. Hopper.

114

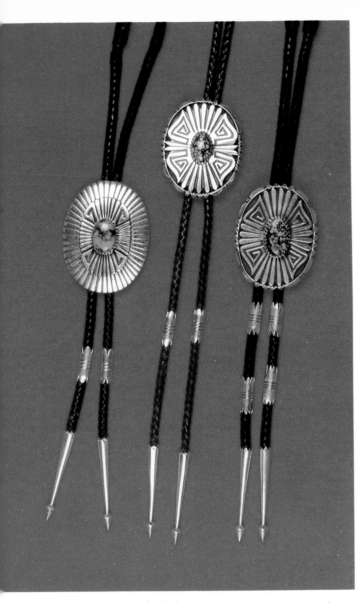

Navajo silversmith Johnny Billie made these three bola tie slides and tips with matrix turquoise stones, c. 1990. Turquoise Lady.

The punch work and silversmithing is of the highest quality on this bola tie slide and tips by Navajo artist Paul Arviso, c. 1990. Turquoise Lady.

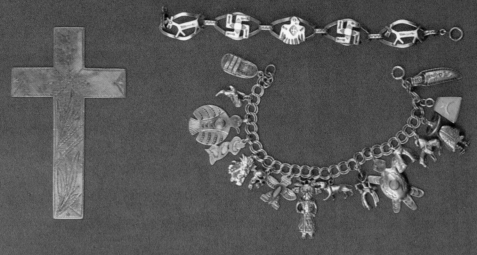

A beautifully engraved cross by a Navajo silversmith would be prized by Christian worshippers. The link bracelet was Navajo-made for the tourist market, c. 1950. The charm bracelet was surely built one charm at a time by a loyal admirer of Southwest culture. **Lynn Trusdell.**

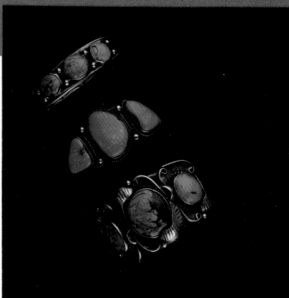

Different turquoise mines are represented by the variously colored stones in these three, Navajo-made, three-stone silver bracelets.

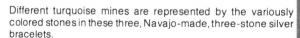

This Navajo-made, silver cross pendant on a hand-constructed silver chain supports turquoise stones from the Kingman mine. B. Hopper.

This fine matching set of silver squash-blossom necklace, bracelet and ring with Pilot Mountain turquoise was made by a Navajo silversmith, c. 1990. Palms Trading Company.

The contemporary squash-blossom necklace and thin line bracelet are traditional Navajo styles. In contrast, the wide cuff bracelet with Kingman turquoise displays the innovative talent of contemporary Navajo silversmith M. Nez, c. 1990. Hogback Trading Company.

The imaginative silver pendant with coral and turquoise stones was constructed by Navajo silversmith Minnie Thomas in 1979. The ring, earclips and naja-shaped pendant were made by Navajos but are not marked.

This graceful finger ring of silver was Navajo-made with Bisbee matrix turquoise in the 1970s. B. Hopper.

The craftsmanship in this contemporary squash-blossom style necklace by Navajo silversmith Charlton Draper is remarkably refined. Turquoise Lady.

119

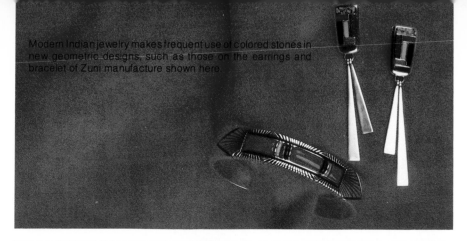

Modern Indian jewelry makes frequent use of colored stones in new geometric designs, such as those on the earrings and bracelet of Zuni manufacture shown here.

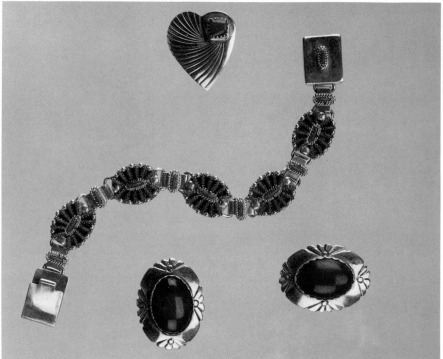

Contemporary Southwest silver jewelry includes some remarkable new designs set with coral. These examples include a Navajo heart-shaped pin, a very fine Zuni needlepoint link bracelet, and a pair of Navajo earclips.

Zuni jeweler Don C. Dewa made this silver and stone inlay bracelet with a sunface design, c. 1990. Beyond Indian Tradition Gallery.

Jewelry designer Robert J. Koeppler emerged in 1962 as a talented silversmith when he won his first competition. Since then, his success and daring have grown to produce very refined designs based on naturalistic and American Indian cultural themes. Jewelry and small boxes have become his specialty. His work continues in Montana and Wisconsin.

The intricate pendant panels of this silver necklace display the early efforts of jeweler Robert J. Koeppler to create depth in his designs. Coral and turquoise stones are inlaid, c. 1975.

The silver pill box "Spring Flower" has a sensitive sculpture of a mother and her child on the top and panels of Montana agate inlaid in the sides. The piece was created by Robert J. Koeppler in 1992. Jean B. Nawodylo. Photography by Cynthia Becker White and William H. Nawodylo.

This extraordinary silver bola tie slide and tips are entitled "The Waiting Game" by their maker Robert J. Koeppler, c. 1990.

Robert J. Koeppler constructed this man's ring with silver and Montana agate from the Yellowstone river, c. 1980. Jean B. Nawodylo. Photography by Cynthia Becker White and William H. Nawodylo.

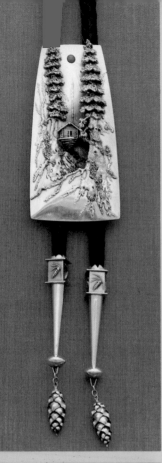

These detailed silver bolo slides were made in 1991 by Robert J. Koeppler. The slide above left he calls "Before the Axe" as a tribute to the magnificent trees that dominate the design. The slide above right he calls "Shadows in the Dark" and it features the coyote he fed for two years which became his model for many designs. Below at left is a bolo slide entitled "Eagles Mate for Life." At the right below, the slide is called "Valley of the Eagles" and its tips include tiny silver mocassins, detailed to the imprint of a foot on the soles. Jean B. Nawodylo. Photography by Cynthia Becker White and William H. Nawodylo.

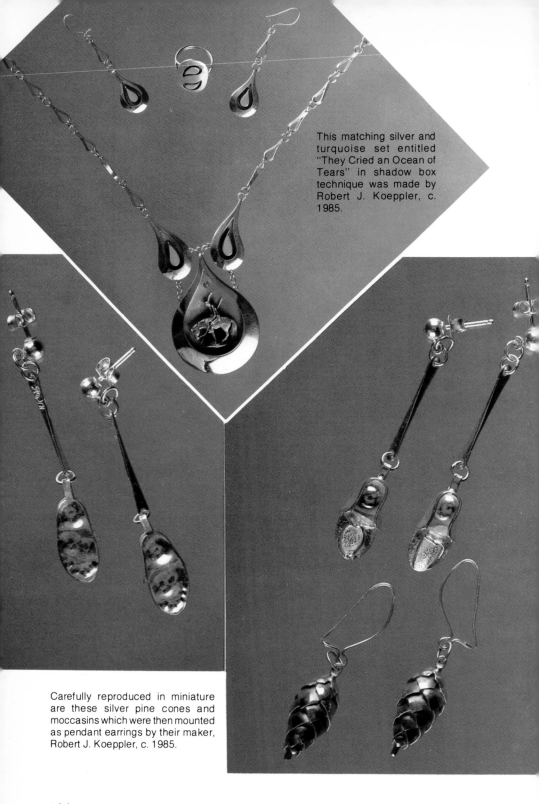

This matching silver and turquoise set entitled "They Cried an Ocean of Tears" in shadow box technique was made by Robert J. Koeppler, c. 1985.

Carefully reproduced in miniature are these silver pine cones and moccasins which were then mounted as pendant earrings by their maker, Robert J. Koeppler, c. 1985.

Finely crafted silver feathers frame the figure in a canoe on this silver pendant and earrings by Robert J. Koeppler, c. 1980.

After working intensely for many weeks without rest, concerned friends warned jeweler Robert J. Koeppler to "stop and smell the roses." He responded by beginning work on this ambitious shadow box design for a scent bottle entitled "Stop and Smell the Roses." Jean B. Nawodylo. Photography by Cynthia Becker White and William H. Nawodylo.

Silver and carnelian have been intricately worked by Robert J.
Koeppler to create this buckle entitled "One for Me," a design
that depicts the competition for survival among a fish, a heron
and a human, c. 1985.

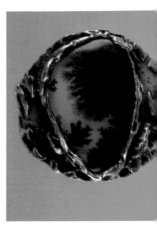

Montana agate is framed in a man's ring of highly personalized
silver design which maker Robert J. Koeppler titled "The
Hound and the Rabbit," c. 1985.

These miniature silver boots were made by Robert J. Koeppler when he demonstrated silversmithing on the Jacquelyn Kennedy Art Train in Michigan in 1978. Jean B. Nawodylo. Photography by Cynthia Becker White and William H. Nawodylo.

The miniature silver stagecoach and buckboard were meticulously constructed in 1983 by Robert J. Koeppler. The wheels on each piece actually turn. Jean B. Nawodylo. Photography by Cynthia Becker White and William H. Nawodylo.

Silversmith Robert J. Koeppler named the design on this belt buckle "Did You Hear the Echo," c. 1985.

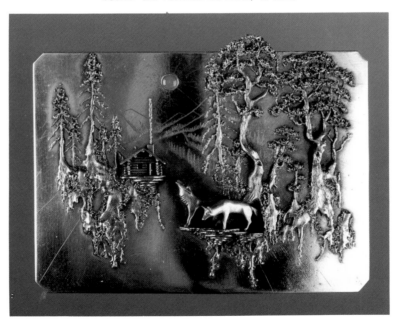

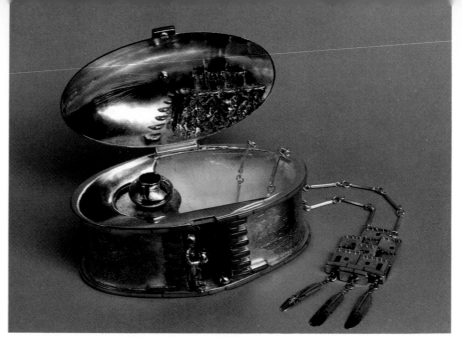

The interior and exterior of this fine silver box are decorated in a design titled "Sands of Time." The lid ornament and accompanying pendant necklace represent pueblo mud houses as found in the villages of the native people in New Mexico and Arizona. The oval box design simulates a mud hogan dwelling similar to those found in the same region on open land. Turquoise and carnelian details and an exquisitely detailed silver figure with pottery bowl forms complete the ornamentation. These were made by Robert J. Koeppler, c. 1985. Ted Garoutte. Photography by Margot Geist.

On the left, the silver and turquoise sculpture "Follow the Wild
Goose" and on the right, the perfume bottle "Fly with the
Eagle," both by Robert J. Koeppler, c. 1990.

Side view of the perfume bottle "Fly with the Eagle," shown
above, with the perfume applicator rod removed.

"Still Waters" silver pill box is Robert J. Koeppler's tribute to Indian canoeists. Designed in 1991, it includes meticulous miniature details of vegetaion and wild life encountered along the waterways. A panel of Montana agate inlaid on one side is further embellished with painted detail. Ted Garoutte. Photography by Margot Geist.

Computer Age

The William de Lillo, Haute Couture House of Jewellery was started in 1967 when jewelry designers William de Lillo and Robert F. Clark teamed up in New York to furnish exceptional and very intricate designs in costume jewelry. Their success was enormous, catering to the most prestigious couture houses in the world. After a ten-year excursion in the south of France to develop their individual sculpture styles, de Lillo and Clark again collaborated in about 1985 to create sculpture-jewelry in precious metals in limited editions. Their inspiration for these designs extends to geometric, cubic and architectural forms and images created by computer graphics. They hope to have created modern designs that relate to the twenty-first century. Their work continues, now in Scottsdale, Arizona.

A sterling silver Ankh, one of civilization's oldest forms, is made new by the mosaic texture of this numbered limited edition series by William deLillo and Robert F. Clark, 4½" long, c. 1985. Wm. de Lillo Archive.

African-made dangle earrings of silver and gold defy time by their direct and simple human design, yet they were new when bought in 1990.

"Concepts in Geometrics" collar of sterling silver and 14kt gold is made with a rigid front and linked back by William de Lillo and Robert F. Clark, front 2½″ high, c. 1985. Wm. de Lillo Archive.

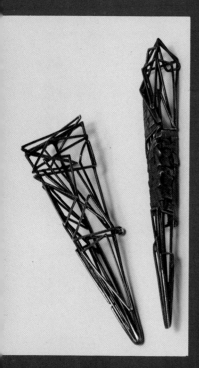

"Architectural Concept" collar of a numbered, limited edition series in oxydized sterling silver, handconstructed by William de Lillo and Robert F. Clark, front 3″ wide, c. 1985. Wm. de Lillo Archive.

Two "Triangles" series brooches handconstructed of oxydized silver by William de Lillo and Robert F. Clark, c. 1985. At left, with 14kt gold, 5½″ long; at right, 6″ long. Wm. de Lillo Archive.

"Geometric" necklace, bracelet and earclips of articulated, sterling silver links in a hammered architectural pattern. The set was handconstructed in a limited and numbered edition by William de Lillo and Robert F. Clark, c. 1985. Wm. de Lillo Archive.

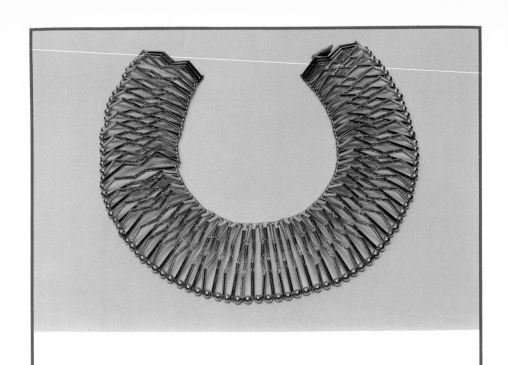

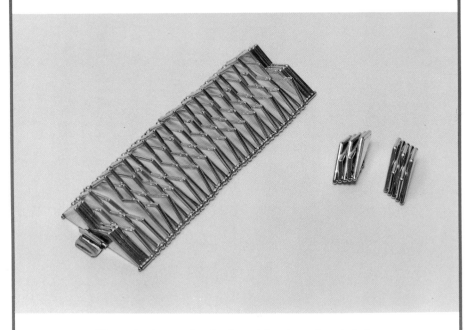

"Computer Imagery" collar, bracelet and earclips of sterling silver geometric sections mounted with silver beads in a design inspired by computer graphic movements. This set was handconstructed in a limited and numberesd edition by Wm. de Lillo and Robert F. Clark, c. 1985. Wm. de Lillo Archive.

"Chevron" necklace, bracelet and earrings of cast and patinated silver made in a limited and numbered edition by William de Lillo and Robert F. Clark, c. 1985. Wm. de Lillo Archive.

"Butterfly" brooch of hand constructed sterling silver, 4¼" long, by William de Lillo and Robert F. Clark, c. 1985. Wm. de Lillo Archive.

"Spider Mask" brooch of oxydized sterling silver handconstructed by William de Lillo and Robert F. Clark, 3¼" long, c. 1985. Wm. de Lillo Archive.

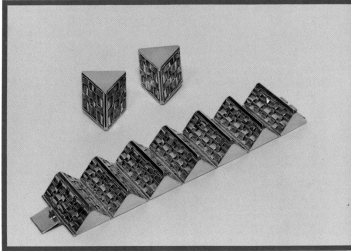

"Prismatic Weave" necklace, bracelet and earclips of articulated sterling silver, hand constructed in limited and numbered edition by William de Lillo and R. F. Clark, c. 1985. Wm. de Lillo Archive.

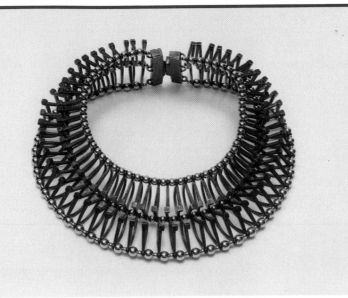

"Computer Technology" necklace, bracelet and earclips made with cast sterling silver bridges and silver beads in a limited and numbered edition. The design was inspired by computer graphic movements and hand made by William de Lillo and Robert F. Clark, c. 1985. Wm. de Lillo Archive.

Price Guide

Values vary immensely according to an article's condition, location of the market, parts of the country, materials, craftsmanship, demand and overall quality of design. While estimates from our survey of different markets may serve as a general guide for evaluation, collectors must use their own judgement and make their own decisions. Values given are in U. S. dollars.

Page	Item	Value range
1	brooch	1500-2000
5	brooches	50-100 ea.
8	pendant	100-175
9	butterfly	95-150
	bracelet	150-225
	flower	75-125
10	bracelets	75-125 ea.
	brooch	50-100
	pendant	75-125
	scatter pins	50-75 ea.
11	brooch	100-200
	bracelet	100-175
	earrings	100-150/pr
	ring	100-200
12	pendant	150-250
	earrings	95-125/pr
13	brooch	100-175
	pendant	100-150
	bead	
	necklace	100-150
	drop earrings	75-100
	bangle	125-175
	drop brooch	100-200
14	disc brooch	50-100
	bracelet	150-250
	turquoise	
	brooches	75-125 ea.
	necklace	125-250
15	belt	250-450
	necklace	120-160
	bracelet	100-150
16	lapis bracelet	750-925
	earrings	150-225
	Napier	
	bracelet	75-125
17	turquoise	
	set	250-400
18	necklace	200-300
19	comb	150-225
	earrings	175-225
20	left tablet	50-100
	center tablet	100-150
	right tablet	75-100
	brooch	50-75

Page	Item	Value range
21	cape chain	50-75
	chatelaine	800-1000
22	needle case	75-100
	letter opener	50-75
	mustache	
	comb	50-75
	cape chain	75-100
	lorgnette	300-500
23	top locket	250-325
	brooch	200-250
	pendant	150-225
	large heart	125-200
	small heart	75-125
	rattle	50-100
	whistle	50-100
24	small	
	brooches	75-150
	Scottish	
	brooch	275-350
	stamp case	75-125
25	buttons	25-45 ea.
	set	200-400
26	sm. cherubs	75-125/pr
	lg. cherubs	100-200/pr
	fish	75-150/pr
	profile brooch	150-250
27	top bar pin	50-75
	center bar pin	65-95
	lady brooch	200-275
	bracelet	225-300
28	parrot	
	pendant	1500-2000
	amazonite	
	pendant	1500-200
	coral brooch	350-500
	leaves brooch	250-400
29	onyx brooch	700-1000
	amethyst	
	brooch	1000-1500
	bracelet	800-1000
30	brooch	150-250
31	necklace	175-275
32	top rings	125-225
	bottom rings	150-300
	cuff	600-900
33	top earrings	75-125/pr

No.	Item	Price
	disc earrings	300-400
	hammered cuff	700-1000
	linked cuff	150-300
34	initial brooches	150-200ea.
	brooches	100-175ea.
35	brooch/pendant	275-350
36	floral brooch	125-175
	pendants	175-225ea.
	safety pin	150-225
	necklace	275-350
37	earrings	150-200/pr.
	brooches	175-475ea.
	necklace	275-350
38	brooches	95-175 ea.
	clips	100-175ea.
	necklace	350-450
	earrings	100-150
39	left necklace	400-500
	right necklace	200-300
40	top earrings	75-125
	bottom earrings	300-375
	necklace	250-400
41	top earrings	
	left	300-375 /pr
	center	250-300/pr
	right	275-350/pr
	below left earrings	
	long dangle	125-175
	right pendants	100-145
	bows	150-200
	pearls	125-165
	hearts	75-100
	flowers	75-100
	jet set	250-400
42	brooch	95-120
	top earrings	75-175/pr
	bottom earrings	100-200/pr
43	rings	150-300ea.
44	concha bracelet	200-400
	amethyst bracelet	300-500
45	top brooches	75-125
	earrings	50-100
	bottom brooches	50-90
	bracelet	75-125
46	earrings	75-125
	brooches	45-90
	buckle	100-150
	bracelets	125-200
47	set	400-600
	bracelet	100-150
48	set	300-550
49	set	300-600
	bracelets	200-300ea.
50	top brooch	75-100
	bracelet	100-175
	earrings	75-100
	agate brooches	75-125 ea.
51	penguin	60-100
	pendant	100-150
	rect. brooch	75-125
	bracelet	150-250
	earrings	75-150 ea.
52	top bracelet	150-250
	head brooch	200-350
	bottom bracelet	150-250
	pendant	100-150
	obsidian bracelet	200-300
53	bracelet	150-225
	necklace	200-300
	silver mask	100-150
	stone mask	150-250
	top ring	100-150
	obsidian ring	100-150
	earrings	100-150
	earclips	75-12/pr
	brooches	50-85 ea.
54	Teran earclips	200-300
55	set	100-175
	openwork bracelet	400-600
	rope bracelet	600-800
56	brooches	100-175ea.
	turquoise set	200-400
57	pin & earrings	125-175
	pin	75-100
58	bracelet	350-450
	set	150-225
59	brooches	250-325ea.
	set	500-700
60	brooch	100-150
	ear drops	75-100
	set	250-350
61	bracelets	150-300ea.
62	set	100-200
	left necklace	150-225
	right necklace	175-275
63	top bracelet	200-175
	bottom bracelet	125-200
	set	125-175
64	necklace	100-150
	brooch	125-175
	earrings	75-100
	set	300-400
65	top brooches	50-100
	bottom brooches	50-125
66	set	200-500
	flag	250-500
	pins & earclips	50-100 ea.
67	flower brooch	150-225
	earrings	75-100
	bow	50-100
	bug	150-200
	bird brooches	150-350ea.
68	bracelet & watch	special
	bar pin	250-350
69	necklace	100-200
	brooch	50-75
	match safe	75-125
	rattle	100-150
	set	125-200
70	set	400-500
	top brooch	75-100
	ship brooch	50-90
71	necklace	200-300
	brooches	125-200ea.
	bracelet	250-350
72	pendant	300-400

No.	Item	Price
	top brooch	90-125
	rect. brooch	200-300
	bottom brooch	200-300
73	brooches	125-250 ea.
	bracelet	175-225
74	top brooches	100-175
	bottom left	100-175
	bow	125-175
	looped brooch	75-125
	floral brooch	125-175
75	necklace	125-175
	earclips	75-125
76	brooches	75-175 ea.
77	top brooches	50-100 ea.
	bottom brooches	50-125 ea.
78	large two hearts	400-600
	small two hearts	150-20
	top bow	100-200
	center bow	150-250
	basket	200-300
	oval	250-350
	bracelet	200-300
79	large basket	450
	large flower	300-400
	bottom round	100-150
	bouquet	125-200
	double bow	300-400
80	bracelet	450-600
	pendant	450-650
81	top brooches	150-250 ea.
	bracelet	200-300
	earrings	100-175
	bottom brooch	250-350
82	set (4 pc)	400-600
83	spray pin	450-600
84	face brooch	250-35
	top set	250-350
	cherub earrings	75-125
	bottom sets	
	left	250-350
	center	275-375
	right	250-350
85	set	400-650
86	rings	150-275 ea.
	bug pins	75-125
	bug earrings	125-175/pr
	large pin	250-375
	wreath pins	100-200 ea.
87	clown	100-175
	large butterfly	250-350
	two butterfly pins	200-350/set
	butterfly earrings	100-175/pr.
88	orchid set	400-600
	rings	100-175 ea.
	brooches	100-175 ea.
	earrings	75-150/pr
89	shield set	500-700
90	top link bracelet	175-300
	charm bracelet	175-275
	belt	800-1200
	bottom bracelet	125-175
91	flower brooches	175-300
	V-eagle	300-700

No.	Item	Price
	key	175-275
	turtle	400-600
92	plaque	75-125
	bracelets:	
	birds	175-225
	pinecones	500-600
	squares	400-500
	swirls	200-300
93	link bracelet	100-150
	set	75-100
	cuff	100-150
94	figural pins	50-100 ea.
95	figural pins	50-100 ea.
96	figural pins	100-200 ea.
	bracelets	100-200
97	set	300-400
98	top charm bracelet	150-250
	rhymes bracelet	125-175
	cut-out bracelet	75-125
	charm bracelet	125-175
99	bracelets	125-250 ea.
100	leaf clip	100-150
	earrings	50-75
	bird	100-175
	flower	100-150
101	top flowers	75-125 ea.
	bottom brooches	75-125 ea.
102	top brooches	50-150 ea.
	Coro brooch	100-150
	bracelet	125-200
103	bracelet	100-175
	necklace	150-200
104	chain	50-100
	top earrings	50-100
	left cuff	125-175
	snake cuff	150-250
	bottom cuff	75-150
	bottom earrings	50-100
105	earrings	50-100
	mesh bracelet	100-175
	braid brooch	75-125
	butterfly	75-150
106	brooch	15-25
	turquoise earclips	50-75
	link bracelet	100-150
	tassel set	75-125
107	ring	75-125
	bracelet	75-125
	necklace	100-150
108	bangle bracelets	100-200
	cuff bracelets	200-400
109	cuff bracelets	100-200
	lg. snake	150-250
	sm. snakes	50-100 ea.
110	bracelets	50-100 ea.
111	top bracelet	50-75
	bottom bracelets	75-125 ea.
112	lg. beads	200-300
	sm beads	300-400
	links	250-350
	bracelets	150-500
113	bracelets	300-600
	comb	100-200

114	top bracelet	300-500
	top belt	100-125
	middle belt	200-250
	bottom belt	300-350
	bottom bracelet	300-50
115	left bolas	150-250
	right bola	350-450
116	cross	special
	link bracelet	200-300
	charm bracelet	150-250
	turquoise bracelets	200-300 ea.
	cross pendant	250-350
117	set	600-800
118	necklace	275-375
	line bracelet	150-200
	cuff bracelet	450-550
119	coral pendant	100-150
	top ring	75-125
	earclips	75-125
	naja pendant	75-125
	bottom ring	75-125
	necklace	450-650
120	top earrings	95-150
	top bracelet	100-225
	heart pin	50-100
	link bracelet	150-250
	earrings	50-100
	bottom bracelet	200-300
121	necklace	400-550
	pill box	special
122	bola	1000-1200
	ring	200-300
123	bolas	1000-1200 ea.

124	set	275-400
	earrings	75-125
125	pendant	200-300
	earrings	50-100
	scent bottle	special
126	buckle	500-750
	ring	300-450
127	shoes	75-100
	stage	100-175
	buckboard	100-175
	buckle	400-500
128	box	special
129	sculpture	special
	bottle	special
130	pill box	special
131	Ankh	900-1200
	earrings	150-200
132	"Concepts" collar	3000-3500
	"Triangles"	1200-1500 ea.
	"Architectural" collar	3500-4000
133	"Geometric" complete set	5000-6000
134	"Computer Imagery" complete set	5000-6000
135	"Chevron" set	3200-4000
	"Butterfly"	1000-1200
136	"Spider Mask"	900-1200
	"Prismatic" set	6500-7500
137	"Computer Tech." complete set	4000-4500

Index

ivory, 11, 20, 28

J. Després, 32
J.S., 10, 52
jade, 32
Jensen, Georg, 68
Jerusalem silver, 64
jet, 32, 41
Joseff of Hollywood, 16

Kingman mine, 116
Kingman turquoise, 118
Koeppler, Robert, 121-130
Kramer of New York, 103

lapis lazuli, 16, 23, 28
lavulite, 52

marcasite, 28, 29, 34, 35-43
Maricela, 55
McClelland Barclay, 92
Mexico, 9, 44, 45, 46, 47, 49, 50,
   51, 52, 53-55, 58-60, 98, 101
   ELNA, 49
   Taxco, 48, 52, 55-56
Monet, 24, 101, 104, 106
Morenci mine, 114
Mr. John Couturier Jewels, 75

Napier, 16, 97, 100, 101, 102,
   105, 107
Navajo, 109-113, 115-120
New York, 103
Nez, M., 118
NOE, 56
Norway, 71-73, 107, 18, 20, 55

obsidian, 52-53
onyx, 29, 41, 47, 52,
   75
openwork, 12-15,

pearl, 8, 62, 27, 42
perfume bottle, 129
Peru, 61

Peruzzi, 75
pill box, 121, 130
Pilot Mountain mine,
   117
Pina, Ysidro Garcia, 55
Portugal, 10

Rebajes, Francisco, 92
Reinad, 67
Renoir of California, 93
repoussé, 16
RMS, 50

Sauteur, 93
scent bottle, 125, 129
Schreiner Jewels, 34
shadow box, 124
Sheffield plate, 7
sterling, 6
Symmetallic silver, 14

Tafoya, Art, 114
Taxco, 48, 52, 55-56
Teran, Salvador, 55
Thomas, Minnie, 119
Thune, 73
turquoise, 50, 10, 17,
   23, 32, 63, 114,
   116, 119, 121, 124,
   128
   Kingman, 118
   Morenci, 114
   Pilot Mountain, 117

U.S. Navajo, 111
USN, 66

Van, 102
VD, 70
Viking Craft, 72

Webster, 69
Whiting and Davis, 104

Zuni, 120